HACK THE ENTREPRENEUR

How to Stop Procrastinating, Build a Business, and Do Work That Matters

JON NASTOR

Thank you for reading. Please use this book to do
work that matters.

ISBN: 978-1519678324

www.hacktheentrepreneur.com

For Sadie and Johanna, I love you both.
Thank you for making life an adventure and
encouraging my madness.

"The only people who don't make mistakes are the ones who don't do anything."
- My Dad a hundred times to me as a kid.

Table of Contents

Foreword

A New Opportunity - Entrepreneurship in the Land of Personal Leadership
by Chris Brogan

The term "entrepreneur" basically shakes out to be a person who puts together a business and takes greater risks (financially) than others involved in that business. It means that you have more skin in the game. To me, there's a huge opportunity here for two reasons.

Reason One: It's Easier Than Before

In the "old days" of just a decade or two ago, to be an entrepreneur cost a lot of money. The path to starting something new required a building, technology, a staff, a lot of licenses and regulations, merchant relationships, and so much more. It was cost prohibitive for the "common human" to be an entrepreneur (or so we all seemed to think).

That's why more people seeking to leave the world of being an employee chose to be a freelancer. To be a freelancer was essentially free. The difference was that freelancers hire on to work on the behalf of other companies, but don't really consider themselves much of an entity unto themselves. They're a fill-in.

How times have changed.

Opportunity one is that you can set up your own business entity for very low dollars. Past the legal structure and the very low cost of setting up a business bank account to handle your merchant transactions, a website can be free or cheap. Marketing can be free or cheap. You don't need a building (unless you do). You might need fewer staff, and you can probably pick up contract help easier than hiring (hey, you get to hire the freelancers now!).

1. It's EASIER to run your own business than ever before, and running your own business means that you're an entrepreneur, not a freelancer, IF you opt to put together your own company with its own values, a mission, a set of goals, and some more meat on its bones beyond a logo and pretty business cards (also low cost these days).
2. Companies and people are more willing to work with small and medium businesses than ever before. Though the hype of "small business being the backbone of America" has been far flung and long lasting, it's a little more TRUE today than it ever has been before.

This leads me to reason two that you might be getting into this kind of journey.

Reason Two: More People Are Willing to Help

What Jon Nastor has put together here is a book full of ideas and insights from himself and many friends. These ideas run the gamut from solid business advice to heartfelt conversations directly to the parts of entrepreneurship that will tear your guts open, if you don't have your head on straight.

Hack the Entrepreneur has a lot of things going for it. The ideas are fast. They come from a place of having recreated this all for the first time (if that makes sense). There's a lot of "We got here a different way, but you're going to like the results" kind of moments in this book.

Simply put: if you're looking to get into entrepreneurship, this is a powerful opportunity to get involved with the thoughts and people that Jon Nastor has put together for you in this book. This is the information that you'd earn after hundreds of "let me pick your brain" cups of coffee with people kind enough (or silly enough) to give you their time and answer your questions. That is, if you even knew half of the questions you have to ask to get yourself moving forward.

What this book will NOT do for you

It's important to be clear with you, dear reader. If you're going to pick up this book (and you've got your eyes on it somehow at the moment or you can't read these words), you're going to have to do the work.

This book will not launch your company for you. This book will not pick up the phone for you and ask a stranger for their hard earned money. It will not have the difficult conversation with your significant other about what this journey will really be like, versus the dream you're trying to sell him or her.

That's your work. Jon Nastor and friends have given you a LOT of tools and thoughts and mindsets to get you on the journey.

YOU have to execute. You have to put forth effort. You have to own your choices here.

But you knew that.

-- Chris Brogan...
CEO, Owner Media Group, Inc
New York Times Bestselling author of *The Freaks Shall Inherit the Earth*

Introduction

I was violently shaking.

Standing on the side of the pool at the age of eight, I was being told to jump straight into the deep end. My swimming instructor, who was in the pool and quickly losing patience with me, expected me to jump, and coerced me.

"I can't do it," I muttered through chattering teeth, "I can't swim." Not only did I not know how to swim, but I was terrified of the water. I couldn't swim – how could she expect me to jump in and swim to the other side of the pool?

As panic riddled my brain, someone ran up behind me and shoved me into the water. I panicked and went under, then regained my sense of time and place. At that point, I flailed my arms and kicked my legs as if my life depended on it. Then it happened.

I began to tread water. Not swim laps, but survive.

No one expects you to jump in and immediately start swimming laps. It's far more likely that you will jump in and flail about. At some point, something will change your life forever and you will begin to tread water.

For an entrepreneur, treading water refers to projects, clients, and freelance work. Those are the first places where we get our feet wet.

This book was written to push you into the pool.

During the early months where you begin to tread water, you will realize (as I did many years ago) that you are not going to drown. You could, in fact, tread water for months or years before you figure out how to swim laps.

This is a phase of entrepreneurship you will want to push past quickly, yet it is the time in your life that you will later look back on with admiration. Like your first kiss or the first concert you went to, your first business is something you never forget. Treading water is your first step towards doing work that matters.

The New Rules of Business

The rules that determined and defined how ideas were brought to market have disappeared.

The rules that said where and when we worked have been replaced with coffee shops and late-night mastermind sessions.

The bank loans to take our ideas to market have been replaced with the $100 startup.

A business that you could run for the rest of your life has been replaced by portfolio businesses – multiple income-generating businesses with you as the only consistent variable.

It wasn't long ago that we were told to go to business school, come up with an idea, get funding, start a business, hire employees, and rent a large office space for said employees to work in.

That is no longer the case.

Business school is not where you go to start a business – it is where you go to learn to work within someone else's business. Maybe that's what you want, or maybe it's not.

Starting a business is how you learn to start a business.

You are not supposed to know the ins and the outs of starting, running, and growing a business. You learn those skills along the way.

Business has fundamentally changed in a way that enables entrepreneurs like us to take action and build significant businesses – only bound by our ambition and desire to be remarkable.

Those changes have opened up the market for us to create and profit under the new school of business. This new school will enable you to reach your goals and live the life that you've been wanting to live – and the best part is, it doesn't involve any "actual" school.

It requires you to think, work, and act boldly.

Welcome to Hack the Entrepreneur

Sitting down over coffee and talking business has always been a passion of mine. Because of that, I have spent a large portion of my working life picking the brains of entrepreneurs who walked the entrepreneurial path before me.

More than 200 interviews and over 1.4 million downloads of the Hack the Entrepreneur podcast later, I want to give you the best hacks. From over 200 conversations, I have chosen the 50 best, not in terms of "big names" – although some of those are definitely in here – but based on what and who will help you move from getting started in business to scaling far beyond your wildest dreams.

This book contains brilliant business insights from the founders of companies with hundreds of employees and $100 millions in revenue, but also from founders that run highly profitable businesses from their laptops as they nomadically travel the world, looking for adventure. Both groups are extremely successful, and both will teach you how business is run under the new rules.

Do not underestimate what you, your laptop, a good wifi connection, and some hard work can accomplish. These are the new rules of business. Get used to it, or keep your day job.

How This Book Will Work for You

This book consists of five parts that have been arranged in a logical sequence to get you unstuck and moving onto each stage.

There are no spare words or chapters in this book; it has been edited down to the bare essentials. You can read it from beginning to end, if you desire, but it is designed to be picked up to help you through whatever it is you are facing in your business today.

Here's how it breaks down:

Getting Started

In this section, I show you what is in your way and how you can work through it. There are similar obstacles we all face or have faced when getting started in business. Once we break through and get started, we wish we could've started sooner. Now you can.

Mindset

You need a mindset shift, which will lead you to doing work that matters to you and to the world.

There are endless tactics and strategies you can use to start and grow your business, but without the proper mindset you will never achieve the level of success you deserve.

This section will help you form that mindset.

Ideas

A lack of ideas is not the reason why we don't endlessly start new projects. The real reason is a lack of resources, time, and energy in our personal lives and organizations. Filtering and implementing those ideas is what matters.

Ideas breed more ideas, so even if you are struggling to come up with a great business idea right now, don't worry: this section has you covered.

Being Wrong

As entrepreneurs, one of our greatest struggles is the fear of being wrong, making mistakes, and failing. This section is laid out to walk you through how to be wrong in your business, as well as how to use your mistakes to learn, grow, and catapult yourself to new heights.

Growth

This section was written to take you from treading water to swimming laps. Once you have mastered the initial four sections, you will be ready to find and enjoy true growth. This is where you, your ideas, and your business will grow and scale way beyond you.

If I had to boil down what makes an entrepreneur a success or a failure, it would be two things.

1. Self-awareness: the ability to step back and clearly understand your strengths as well as your weaknesses.
2. Mindset: if you are looking to take the easy way out, entrepreneurship is not for you. Being an entrepreneur is a constant path of enormous highs and exhausting lows. Your mindset needs to be honed if you are to succeed. This book is about that mindset.

What This Book Is Not

This is not a book of business tactics or strategies that will become useless in a few months as new technologies emerge. You will not learn how to set up a website or how to source products overseas. You will not be shown new management philosophies or how to become an expert in social media.

There are countless books that cover all of those topics. This book is different.

This book was written to develop you, the entrepreneur. It will introduce you to brilliant entrepreneurs that can teach you great things.

Now, let's get started.

Part I:

Getting Started

Getting Unstuck

I live in the cold, harsh climate of Northern Ontario, Canada. My American friends can't believe anyone could live in the brutally cold and hostile environment of Minneapolis, MN – drive six hours directly north and you will find me (at least for part of the year).

This isn't a geography test or a lesson in climatology; it's about the physical version of being stuck and finding the motivation to get started.

This is where your excuse for not being in the right time or place to start a business goes out the window. You don't need to be in Silicon Valley, New York, Beijing, London, or Barcelona to start, build, and grow an incredibly profitable business that changes your life and that of the people around you.

As long as you have an internet connection and a willingness to do work that matters, where you are right now is where you need to be. You have everything that you need at your disposal – it is completely up to you what you do with it.

The Mental Battle

When I talk about getting unstuck, I am referring to the mental battle of overcoming anything that holds us back from creating cool things. The "getting started" part.

For years, I was under the impression that, in order to be successful, you had to always be productive. If you weren't, then you could not and would not succeed. Now I know this isn't true, but it held me back for far too long.

I would compare myself to people who always seemed to be on their game, working hard at creating cool things and building audiences. Since I didn't always feel "on", I felt I was not cut out for entrepreneurship. However, I learned that was not true for me, and it is not true for you either. The world does not need you to become the next Elon

Musk or Richard Branson – what it needs is you. You are an entrepreneur.

Overcoming my sense of inadequacy was one of the most liberating feelings in my life. It set me on a path to being happier. I have never been more fulfilled by my business and the life I have built around it.

I am not talking work/life balance. I am talking conscious lifestyle design. Everything you've been taught about education, entrepreneurship, and the constant state of consuming other people's products, is a vicious cycle stopping you from doing the work that matters. It is time to start being deliberate in your actions.

Yes, of course you have to find your periods of hustle and hard work, but you also have to nurture your periods of stepping back and taking time off from business. Allowing yourself this time, without becoming anxious you are not working enough, will give you the energy and focus required to build and launch your next project, and grow your business.

This Is Our Beatlemania

I grew up dreaming of being a kid in the '60s and witnessing Beatlemania first hand, but this was not to be. Instead, you and I have been given something much more powerful to be a part of.

The field has been leveled and the barriers to entry have been torn down.

Every day people are living inspired lives built upon their art, their passions, and their ideas – not because someone gave them permission, but because they decided that this was their time and they weren't going to be satisfied if they missed it.

It is no longer a question of whether they will *let* you. It is simply, will you?

We live in a time and place where you have the power to control your future. Today, you could start a blog in less than ten minutes, write a post that resonates with a few people, and through social media be read by more people than a post published by *The New York Times*. Seems unlikely, doesn't it? Yet it happens almost every day.

Under the old rules, *The New York Times* would never publish your article without you having the Old World credentials that they deemed necessary, so your story could easily go untold.

Luckily, we live in the New World, in which we can write our own stories and control our platforms. We no longer need approval, so don't wait for someone else to tell you to start.

However, if that is what you are waiting for...

Start.

The Path of Unpredictability

"I had known I wanted to start a company for a while, but it's difficult to walk away from a paycheck. It was a hard decision that took me longer than I would have liked.

It was easy to see how I could be making more money working for bigger, more established institutions, so I drew two lines to compare.

I drew a line of stability and predictability at a high level of income, where I would be if I had stayed in the path I was in. I then drew a second, lower line that would be what I could expect as an entrepreneur: bootstrapping a company, not paying myself a salary for a few years trying to make ends meet, and with more uncertainty in the long term."

– Jon Stein, founder of Betterment

This is not the type of thing that I would do, but it might be just what you need.

Jon is analytical, so he modeled and planned two potential paths. On the one hand, there is the path of stability with high-paying and powerful jobs, which is predictable. He knew where it would end up and was not entertained by it. On the other hand, there is the path of bootstrapping a company.

Jon didn't just found a small company in an easy market, but stayed in the world of banking and investments. Even though that is an incredibly difficult market, he knew it was the right place for him. He could afford to bootstrap a company for a few years without paying himself a salary, and was still comfortable with the whole idea.

I often advise people to follow their gut, quit their job, and do whatever they feel they have to do. Jon's analytical approach is completely different and is useful for people who need plans.

It is crucial to know that there are different paths to the same end. As different as Jon's tactic is from mine, I like it. I love the fact that his perspective is so different from mine and a lot of my guests'. Most of us follow our gut, but Jon decided to think it through.

There is no right or wrong approach – just follow the method that feels right to you. We have to figure out for ourselves what will shift our mindset in order to take the leap.

Become comfortable being uncomfortable.

Let Your Challenges Become Your Super Powers

"At school, I was immature and impulsive. I was always getting into dangerous things. I was a daydreamer. I got kicked out of school, dropped out, and didn't get into university.

All those things that got me in trouble at school have been the biggest contributing factors to my success today. I remember my teacher writing a letter to my mom, listing all the problems that I had, and I realize now that those problems are actually my strengths.

When you become an entrepreneur, all the challenges you had in schooling become your super powers."

– Dominic Johnson-Hill, founder and Creative Director of China's first streetwear clothing brand, Plastered T-Shirts

This quote contains two important elements: schooling and our imperfections growing up.

Your flaws made you stand out and meant that maybe you weren't perfectly normal. It's okay not to be normal – it's cool. You have to think of those traits as you: they are who and what you are. Don't try to change those things, but emphasize them instead. You are all it takes to be awesome.

According to Dominic, our flaws turn into super powers when we become entrepreneurs. Dominic was constantly distracted and disruptive in the classroom, much to the disdain of his teachers, who took this to mean Dominic would never be successful – put simply, he'd never make a good employee. Being disruptive in a classroom is not tolerated, but in business it is a super power. Being disruptive is a path to moving markets and changing the world.

We aren't born entrepreneurs, we become them. I hope I've made that clear. Some of us just step up, call ourselves entrepreneurs, and start building cool stuff.

That's really all there is to it, and I love the way Dominic puts it. Because after someone starts creating stuff, it's easy to look back and say, "Oh, wow, she's an entrepreneur." Was she before? It doesn't matter. She is now. Dominic is a great example, because he is truly entrepreneurial in his lifestyle and actions.

In order to be an entrepreneur, you need to act like an entrepreneur. That means acting however you want, as long as you build things and put them out into the world.

Don't Do What You Love

> "I don't believe people should actually do what they love. You have to learn to love what you do, versus trying to do what you love. I love playing video games, but I wouldn't be proud to say that's what I did for a living."
>
> **– Kate Matsudaira, founder of Popforms**

Many people make the mistake of founding a business based on their passion. You will often hear that you should find out what you love and go into that as a business. There are two things wrong with that.

First of all, your passion might be video games, but that doesn't necessarily mean video games are the right place for you to make money.

Secondly, if you start building a business based on your absolute passion, you will find that you start to dislike what you loved because it has become work.

I love to play drums and I love to travel, but I didn't make a business around either of those things. I built a business around software that helps fix issues people are having. That business makes me money, which I can use to buy the time and freedom to travel with my family.

Rather than building a business around what you love, build a viable business that gives you the money and freedom to do what you love.

Businesses Are Like Software

"Businesses are like software. A little work invested early on in designing things to create the outcomes you want is a lot easier than retrofitting those outcomes onto a complex system that's already moving and needs to continue moving, or else it will explode."

— Patrick MacKenzie, co-founder and CEO of Starfighter

People spend a lot of time planning the outcomes of their choices, be it exercising, dieting, or vacations. Yet they fail to do so when building a business.

The key is to focus on what you want to get out of your business and set it up accordingly early on. Maybe we feel this is unattainable because we focus on growth so much.

Patrick has built a business strictly around the lifestyle he wants. He has given up money and business growth to ensure his business is built and run the way he wants it to be. That is the definition of a lifestyle business.

Personally, I run my multiple businesses with partnerships and freelancers to leverage my time and impact. On the surface, this could be seen to hamper the growth of my businesses, but I consciously decide to only build businesses that will leave a lot of time and freedom for the things that I really love to do.

Don't get me wrong, I love creating and growing businesses, but there is nothing more valuable to me than my time. It may change at some point, and that's okay, but for now this is what works.

What do you want your lifestyle and businesses to look like? Think about this when starting, and begin with your end goals in mind.

Once you build a business of one hundred employees, it's really hard to go back. Not that it's wrong – if that's what you want to do, by all means. However, it is a good idea to think about these thing beforehand.

When creating our first businesses, we often have a tendency to set up the wrong foundation. There are several explanations for that: we may think of our businesses in the traditional sense, or we simply feel that having an office, employees, fancy logos, and a custom website will validate our businesses to ourselves, our families, and our friends. Unfortunately, more times than not, this is the faulty foundation that destroys our business.

Determine exactly what you want from your business. Then begin with the end in mind.

Be a Painkiller, Not a Vitamin

> "Every company needs to solve a problem, which you can compare to the function of a painkiller as opposed to a vitamin. When we have a toothache, we want a painkiller, not a vitamin, and we're willing to pay for it."
>
> **– Matt Barrie, founder and CEO of Freelancer.com**

Does it get any simpler than that? If your business solves a problem that your customer is experiencing, then you are their painkiller. The customer will immediately need your assistance.

This is the difference between creating a product that people want and a product that people need. When we are in some sort of pain, we need a painkiller as soon as possible. We are less price-sensitive and less likely to shop around. When you can position your product like this, you will have an enormous advantage.

I love the simplicity of Matt's approach: "Be a painkiller, not a vitamin." If you offer a service that people are in need of, they will happily pay for it.

Entrepreneurs Are Not Born

> "I have a confidence about myself as a human being. Just appreciate that wherever you're at, you're a whole and complete human being with everything you possibly need to be successful. You deserve to achieve, and you deserve the fruits of your labor."
>
> **— Landon Ray, founder and CEO of Ontraport**

As we gain success, we sometimes think we don't deserve it. Prior to that stage, we might read books by "famous" or established entrepreneurs, whom we consider to be natural born entrepreneurs. There is no such thing as being born an entrepreneur.

We all have it in us to step up and achieve things, as long as we are willing to do the work. We have to be aware that our every success and our position in life spring forth from our own actions and efforts. We deserve our wins and our losses. We deserve to do big, cool things.

There is not a huge difference between the smartest person and the dumbest person in the world. Similarly, I don't believe there is a big difference between the very successful and the unsuccessful. The largest difference is that the successful, famous people are the ones who want to be successful. They know they deserve it and push until they achieve it.

The hardest part of doing big things is convincing yourself that you can.

The rest is just work.

What's Holding You Back?

"The pattern in my own entrepreneurial life is finding outside forces or outside pressure to help me take action.

In the beginning, I had to find out what excuse was holding me back, and how I could stop using that excuse. I ended up hiring someone really affordable to help me build the bones and teach me WordPress, and I had a blog built. It was ready to go – I had no more excuses and just had to start writing.

You have to find a way to overcome your excuse for not getting started."

**– Stephanie Halligan, artist and
founder of Art to Self**

Stephanie had no more excuses once she had her blog built. She was using her lack of technical knowledge as an excuse, which she chose to overcome by hiring somebody for a price she could afford. This was neither expensive nor difficult, but it wiped out her excuse.

She forced herself to start.

It seems so simple: the key is to overcome your own barriers. It doesn't matter if you're just getting started, creating your first product, making your first podcast, or looking for your first mastermind group. Everyone has their own barriers that they can't seem to overcome.

Remove your barriers.

You are the only one who can figure out what they are. They're never as big as you make them out to be, especially if you break them down into smaller pieces.

Here's what to do: figure out what your barriers are, overcome them immediately (on your own or with someone's help), and invalidate your excuses.

It is important to get through them and move on, because all the time you spend being stuck is time that you could be using to do big things. After all, they're just excuses.

We always overestimate the size of our hurdles, until we overcome them.

It Will Never Be Worse Than Today

"We count our achievements too soon. Some people think they will be rich on the first day their website is online.

There is a much better perspective: the first day your website is up, it will look the worst that it is ever going to look. It's the worst product offering you'll ever have, because you will keep improving it from there."

– Andrea Lake, founder of StickerJunkie and Delinquent Distribution

From the moment we launch something, whether it's a product, a podcast, a blog, or a new service, we want it to be perfect. So perfect that it typically doesn't even get launched, because it never lives up to our expectations.

Accept that the starting point is the worst your business will ever be.

The beginning of HacktheEntrepreneur.com was hilarious. I paid $125 for a design on 99designs and put it up with my friend Nick Davis over a weekend. It did exactly what it needed to do, though it looked pretty bad. My first episodes were not that great either. Now, one year later, the site is a thousand times better. Similarly, the first version of Velocity Page that we released was terrible. It's only now becoming quite good, because we've iterated and built off the original product. That's how it has to be.

We often think something is a failure, even when we've only just started. Be willing to suck at the beginning. Be aware that you have to progressively get better.

Feel comforted by the knowledge that whatever you do or publish today is the worst it will ever be. You will continue to nurture and improve it. Don't try to make it perfect before putting it out, because you probably won't succeed. On the contrary, you'll become overwhelmed, get caught in a weird cycle of looking for a perfection that never comes, and fail to ever launch.

Today is the worst your business will ever be.

Everyone's Business Is a Mess (at First)

"It might seem like I have my shit together, but by all means, no. When we first started, it was definitely nowhere near as organized: it was just me and my graphic designer. Now we are still all over the place."

– Nathan Chan, founder of *Foundr Magazine*

I'm very happy Nathan mentioned this, because from the outside it does look like he has it all together. In a way, he does, because he has been investing time in his business for more than 1.5 years now. That is a long time to focus on optimizing a business, improving it, and helping it grow.

When talking to people with amazing businesses, it is easy to think they are very far ahead of you. However, bear in mind that they have all been where you are today.

As Andrea Lake pointed out in the previous hack, every time we start something, we have to be aware that at the beginning it is the worst it will ever be.

When Nathan launched *Foundr*, it was a mess, but now things are going well. He's turned it into a real, legitimate business, which makes it seem like it has always been well-organized, even though that's not the case. Initially, the whole business came down to him doing everything.

It is perfectly fine if that is how you are running your business right now. It is okay if everything is disorganized, as long as you are aware that at some point you will have to step up and become the CEO. Being the CEO is impossible in the beginning.

At first you will need to do everything and be every part of your business, even the parts you aren't good at. Your job as an entrepreneur is to work hard, uncover your weaknesses, and slowly delegate jobs out to others, while moving yourself into the role of CEO.

There will always be someone ahead of us, with a better-organized, well-marketed, and growing business. However, that is not important. Every day our business is at the worst point it will ever be, as long as we continue to look and push forward.

Regardless of your current situation, good or bad, rest assured that nobody else has it figured out – no matter how it may look from outside.

What Price Are You Willing to Pay?

"As soon as you find what you really want to do with your life, which is the first challenge, then you have to decide how much you really want it. You always have to pay a price – what is yours?"

– Joanna Penn, self-published *The New York Times* and *USA Today* authorpreneur

At some point you will realize how badly you want the business or lifestyle that you are dreaming of, and what sacrifices you are willing to make. You cannot avoid making sacrifices, whether it is seeing less of your friends, spending less time with your family, or giving up your job security. There is no other way to end up on the other side of the hurdle.

Every successful person will tell you of the struggles and the things they have given up to get to where they are. There is no way around it, and you have to want something bad enough to be willing to make those sacrifices. That's the only way to do it.

You have to know this in advance and be willing to make sacrifices, because the Internet gives us the freedom to do amazing and beautiful things. It is a powerful tool: everyone with a laptop is almost on equal ground, whereas 20-30 years ago giant media companies controlled all the possibilities. Those were the days of permission. Permission is no longer required.

I am a guy sitting in my house with a software business, an online training site, and two podcasts which go out to tens of thousands of people all the time, because I am willing to sacrifice and do the work. You need to want it bad enough. And when you do, you will get it.

Life is short. Do work that matters.

Movement and a Compass

There are no maps for your destination. In order for a map to work, you need to know exactly where you are going – and you don't, can't, shouldn't.

Point A straight to point C, without passing point B, doesn't exist.

Something always comes up, gets in your way, and proves your initial thoughts or ideas wrong. You need to accept that and use it to your advantage, or else you will starve yourself of your true potential.

You are lost in the middle of a forest without food, water, or an idea of what direction you are heading.

What are the two things that could help you most in this situation?

Movement and a compass.

If you stay in one spot because you don't know what your next step should be, you will die. You can't let the pressure of ignorance and disorientation keep you from moving towards salvation.

Let me ask you a question.

Have you ever felt so stuck that you might as well be in the middle of a forest without water and food? I have. I have felt that in the pit of my stomach, and I work every day to never have that feeling again.

When lost in a forest without a compass, you will walk in circles and end up back where you started. It is essential that you start moving, because that is the only way to get anywhere.

With the help of a compass you can pick a direction, based on your most educated guess, and head that way. Pick a direction based on everything you know at this moment, not what you will know next week or month.

Your water is gone – you don't have time to put movement off any longer.

Here's what happens when you start moving: a river, road, or mountain crosses your path. A river and a road you can follow – you may even be able to hitch a ride.

If you hit a mountain that you didn't know was there in the beginning, you now know that you need to try a different direction. That is not a setback, but excellent information that tells you what direction not to go, which is just as important as knowing what direction to go.

This is exactly how you need to direct your life and business.

You will never have all the information, only the information that is available to you where you presently are.

As you move and gain momentum, more opportunities and information will present themselves. Opportunities and information that will never be available back where you started.

Momentum breeds momentum.

Movement will lead you to a far better place than you ever could have found on a map being read by an old version of yourself, the one that was lost in the middle of a forest.

It is time to start walking.

Pick a direction and walk until you find solid evidence that you should alter your path. Oh, and don't forget your compass.

Part II:

Mindset

Move From Consumer to Producer

We spend our entire lives consuming products and services. We want new phones, clothes, and cars. We buy apps and music without even contemplating the purchases – which is great for the producers.

Producers create every app, song, video, phone, website, podcast, and article of clothing that you own or use – and they get paid to do it.

All of us are here because we want to build something out of nothing. We want to create, inspire, and get paid so we can buy the time and freedom to do the things we love to do. In short, we want (and need) to be producers.

Consumers pay for producers to live bold, exciting lives on their own terms. The Internet itself was built by people like you and me. Every time you visit a website today, think about the people that made it from the perspective of a producer.

Move from being a consumer to being a producer.

Being a producer does not mean you can no longer consume goods, but it does affect how you see and interact with those goods. Every website you visit was made by someone like you, except they decided to become a producer. They are not smarter or better than you, but they did step up to produce.

Being a producer is not for everyone. My gut tells me that it is for you.

As a producer, you should think about the people behind every purchase you make. Think about the lives they live due to their decision to produce rather than simply consume.

Producers do not have to learn to design and code – unless code and design is what you produce. Producers need to take an idea and turn it into reality. Create something out of nothing – that is your job as a producer.

The producer of your favourite TV show does not hold the camera and edit the final show. She simply takes an idea and organizes the right people around her to create the best final product possible.

I don't want to oversimplify this point, but it really is just a mindset shift that needs to take place within you. This new mindset will lead you to doing work that matters to you and to the world.

This is just the beginning, and I cannot wait to see what you produce.

Your Losses Will Lead to a Win

"You have to be resilient and able to continue building what you believe is the next best thing. Things you build will often not succeed, but ultimately, those losses will add up to a win, based on what you've learned."

– Todd Garland, founder of BuySellAds

When you build something and put it out there, it very rarely takes off and goes viral.

Todd didn't suddenly overcome his struggles, create BuySellAds, and start earning ten million dollars a year. The process took seven years and was full of struggles, hardship, and things not working the way they were supposed to. Those struggles are never a reason not to build a business – they are necessary to achieve the success of ten million dollars a year.

Not only are highs and lows necessary – they should be the reason why you do it. There is no avoiding struggle and success. To truly find success and happiness in this game of entrepreneurship, you need to enjoy the journey.

Nobody is trying to fail, but it's a necessary evil that will push you, allow you to learn, and help you figure out where you are supposed to go.

There is a story of a great king who asked his royal jeweler to make a ring, engraved with a statement on it that would be true in any circumstance. After much thought, the wise jeweler gave the ring to the king with the inscription, "This too shall pass".

Enjoy the lows, because they make the highs much higher.

Three Steps Ahead

"I follow my gut. I don't play chess, but I imagine that if I did, I would think of every opportunity three steps ahead in every possible direction.

Even if it seems like something would benefit me now, it might not benefit me in the long run. Because I don't have a business background, I check my gut and say, 'Okay, even though it feels good today, it could wind up going down the wrong path, so let's not do it.'

I never thought I'd be an entrepreneur. I didn't even know how to spell 'entrepreneur' when I started."

– Jessie Shternshus, founder of The ImprovEffect and co-author of the book *CTRL Shift: The Book for Any Day*

I love the comparison between entrepreneurship and playing chess. You always have to think three steps ahead. Don't just ask yourself, "What is happening right now?" but, "What will happen three steps from the action that I'm going to take today?"

Obviously, you won't be successful if you expect one thing to be the big entrepreneurial lottery in which you're the winner.

Rather, you have to think longer term and have a vision of where you want to be.

You have to follow your gut. If something seems like it could potentially make you some money now, ask yourself if it's good for you and your customer, or whoever it is that you are serving. If it's not good for them, as well as for you, in the next three steps, then don't do it. It won't help your business grow, and it won't make you successful three steps down the road.

So how can you think three steps ahead when you aren't even sure what your next step is? Good question.

Remember, your business is not about you. It is never about you. It is about your customer. Starting today, you need to figure out what your customer needs or what transformation you can help them make in their life. Once you determine exactly what this is for your customer, then and only then can you use this as your guide.

Always think beyond today.

Do the Hardest Thing

> "The hardest thing is usually the thing that you should be going after. Chances are that nobody else is, or at least very few people are. Personally, I feel comfortable and even thrive when I don't have a clue what I'm doing."
>
> **– Josh Pigford, founder of Baremetrics**

It is essential that you get used to the uncomfortable feeling of not knowing what you're doing. Whether it's getting on stage to speak, launching your product, or writing a book, we tend to see others doing it and (falsely) assume that they've always been good at it. We all have to do everything for the first time, and none of us do anything very well the first time.

We tend to avoid the things we are not good at, simply because we are not good at them. Unfortunately, this is a self-fulfilling prophecy. If we never do the things we are not good at, how will we ever get good?

It's true, we don't need to be good at everything. However, many of the things we want to be good at take doing them over and over again until we have mastered them. The problem is that we don't want to do things we aren't good at.

How do you do something confidently when you are self-consciously aware that you are no good at it?

Pretend You're Good At It.

Don't discard this idea – it truly works if you take it seriously. Pretending you are good is what people we admire do. They seem masterful, but they are pretending. Seriously.

This is the only way to become good at anything.

Pretending you are good at something will allow you to do it confidently enough times until, guess what? You become good at it.

When you were a kid, you learned that you couldn't get good at something unless you practiced and practiced. Yet, somehow, as we become adults we tend to stop wanting to practice things we are not good at.

We stop growing. We stop learning. We live unfulfilled lives.

I want you to consciously decide to do one thing you are not good at. Not only do it, but pretend you are good at it. Pretend you are a complete natural at whatever it is you need to learn.

Do it confidently and know that if you pretend well enough, anyone watching will simply think you are good at it – you may even think you are good at it too. Or maybe you are?

This simple change in your mindset will allow you to learn and master the things that have always frightened you.

Now, go forth and pretend.

Know Enough to Be Dangerous

"As entrepreneurs we need to know enough to be dangerous in every area. If someone who isn't good at their job crosses our path, we have to be able to recognize that. That's part of what creates these long days: we need to learn all aspects of the business. If we don't, it is hard to delegate, because we won't know what is good and what is bad."

— Michael Sacca, co-founder of WithCircle and host of *Rocketship.FM*

Knowing enough to be dangerous gives us the leverage points we need. It is very hard to outsource something if you know nothing about it.

Yes, do the things you are good at and outsource the rest, but don't use that as an excuse to not learn about the essential aspects of your business.

As the owner, you are the captain of your ship, so you need to take responsibility for everything that happens, good or bad. How can you possibly do that if you don't learn how to steer?

Don't listen to the experts who tell you that you should only do a tiny bit of your business and outsource the rest. There's no such thing as a four-hour work week and being able to outsource everything, especially not at the beginning.

Obviously, we don't need to be accountants, lawyers, and editors all-in-one, but we have to know enough to be dangerous.

You have to dive in head first and learn everything there is to learn about your business. Then, when you get lucky and have that momentum, you can take the revenue you've created, take all the bits of knowledge you have, and put people in place to take care of those things. Bear in mind, though, that it's still your business and you are still responsible for it.

Be knowledgeable. Be dangerous.

Determine Your Why

"Everyone is talking about success, money, and results, but you can also do something that just makes you happy. For example, someone else can code a webpage for me, but doing it just makes me happy, and I want to get really good at it. The reason I got very good at writing articles was not that I was a good writer, but that I was determined to become a good writer."

– Sean D'Souza, co-founder of PsychoTactics and author of *The Brain Audit*

We always talk about delegating everything so we can focus on the important things. However, success, money, and results may not be the most important things to you. Time is my most important metric, because it is a non-renewable resource.

We can focus on building massive businesses and realize they have consumed our lives, or we can focus on building lifestyle businesses. I personally focus on the latter: I have a business that gives me the lifestyle I want without having to work all the time. I don't want to create myself a job – I want to create a business that provides me with the freedom to travel, hang out with my family, play the drums, and do cool projects.

It's awesome if you want to build a hundred-person team and take over your market, but do not think that it is necessary.

Don't let fate determine what kind of business you will end up with. Decide where you want to be, and then work backwards.

If you want to get really good at something, you have to do it yourself, instead of outsourcing it. It is fine that it takes you ten times as long in the beginning. Sean mentions writing because he offers a writing course to people. I love how he clarifies that he was not a good writer, but he simply loved doing it and worked at it until he *became* a good writer.

This is the growth mindset as opposed to the fixed mindset.

The fixed mindset tells you that you can't learn, get smarter, or become better at things, because the skills and knowledge you are born with or without certain skills and knowledge.

The growth mindset tells you that if you put in the work and the time, you can master anything and simply do it for fun, because you love it. That is a meaningful clarification in the world of business.

Do what makes you happy.

Create Your Own Luck

"So-called lucky people aren't necessarily getting more advantages than other people. The universe doesn't favor them, but they're putting themselves out there more. They're creating more connections that could lead to other stuff. That is really how I interpret luck: creating more of a mathematical probability that you're going to get what you want."

– Russ Perry, founder of Design Pickle

Luck's a funny thing, isn't it? As Russ says, it is about creating a mathematical probability by putting yourself out there and trying more things. When you start a business, it might fail. You might have to create ten businesses before one will be successful. From a personal perspective, nothing frustrates me more than people telling me I am lucky. We make our luck with the decisions we make and the actions we take. Plain and simple.

Certain people around me were not supportive when I started to build my business five years ago. I had less time to hang out with them, and they couldn't understand why I would spend time working on my own projects after coming home from my job. However, now that I do not have to work as much and have the opportunity to travel the world, those same people tell me, "Wow, Jon, you're so lucky." Am I, or did I get here by working my ass off?

We can put ourselves in the way of luck, so it can find us. You have to make yourself lucky.

The world will conspire to help you achieve your goal if you put yourself out there more, write more, start more businesses, build more apps, do more artwork, and go to more conferences. Whatever it is you do, do more of it than you're already doing. Trust me, as Russ says, you can create a mathematical probability for luck. It's a misconception that you are born with a horseshoe stuck somewhere that doesn't even sound lucky at all.

Luck is a by-product of hard work.

How to Create Amongst Chaos

"For me, right now, life does not feel like something that has to be balanced, but like a tension that has to be managed. Most of my life is figuring out how to create amidst chaos.

I had the weird idea that once I quit my job, I would have a lot of time to write. Somehow, magically, all the time that I thought I'd spend writing got filled with doing other activities. That is especially the case if you want to figure out the blend of being an artist and entrepreneur, or being creative while making money.

Those people will experience a weird tension between, on the one hand, honing their craft and growing, and on the other hand, connecting with people and building a community.

– Jeff Goins, digital entrepreneur and author of
The Art of Work

Everyone will say that balance is important, but for Jeff life isn't something that needs to be balanced right now. It's a tension that he needs to deal with. Not a tension that needs to be endured, but one that needs to be enjoyed.

I am glad he started his statement with "for me", because that is how you can approach this issue. I can tell you how every guest on my show works, thinks, and deals with struggles. However, you cannot simply adopt their technique – you have to find the ones that work for you and confidently go in that direction. Experts and other entrepreneurs will often tell you what works for them, but that does not necessarily mean it will work for you too.

This chaos or tension that we struggle with as entrepreneurs is a necessary part of our journey. Creating something out of nothing and putting it out into the world is never going to be easy. Then again, the goal of life is not ease, it is pushing yourself to the heights you are capable of reaching. You need to become comfortable with the uncomfortable tension and learn to thrive within it.

It is interesting how Jeff thought that once he quit his job everything would change, but it didn't. If you are looking for a sure-fire way to be unhappy, always look ahead and think that when you get "there" (wherever that is), you will be happy.

Be happy with the chaos and enjoy the journey.

Write Down Your Fears

Goals can be very limiting: once you reach a goal, you have nothing left to strive toward. Your fears, on the other hand, are at the basis of an intrinsic problem: why are you not taking action on your ideas, starting a business, or going towards your goals? The answer is usually that you are scared, because there is a multitude of aspects you don't know the first thing about.

I run a software company, but I don't know how to make software and I'm not technically savvy. In fact, my daughter often rolls her eyes in frustration when she watches me try and download an app to my phone.

If I had let my fears hold me back, I would still be doing energy audits, which was my job before I became an entrepreneur. I had to go and check houses for energy efficiency, which meant a long commute and longer work hours. Now I get to stay at home with my family and work. The reason we don't do things is not that we didn't set the right goals – it's that we are afraid.

I have a piece of paper, a "fears page" if you will, where I write down whatever is keeping me from doing something at a specific moment. By doing so, I can dimensionalize my fears, as Jay said. This has allowed me to see what mistakes I have made and how limiting fears can be.

Don't write down your goals, but write down your fears. Then overcome them.

Work to Close The Gap

"The gap is what's between today's goal and the horizon. If you look back at your achievements and consider how far you've come, you will stay out of the gap. However, if you're always walking toward the horizon, without turning around and recognizing your goals as you achieve them, you will never feel fulfilled."

– Brian Kurtz, serial direct marketer and entrepreneur

The idea of the gap was brought to my attention by Brian, but he himself learned it from Dan Sullivan. As entrepreneurs, we have a tendency to set a goal, accomplish that goal, and immediately set five other loftier ones in its place. We do this without ever taking the time to stop, turn around, and see what we have accomplished to get to where we are today.

Even if you are just getting started, think back six months or a year and consider how much more you know today than you did back then. It's true, isn't it? Yes, we still need to set goals in order to continue to grow, but it is essential to close that gap.

Accept that where you are today is a place worth appreciating and celebrating.

The future needs goals, today needs appreciating, and yesterday needs to be acknowledged.

Time is precious. We need to make sure to take the time to stop and look around.

It's an amazing accomplishment to work towards something in order to better yourself and your family. Spend more time contemplating how far you have come. It is tempting to think that you first need to accomplish a certain result. However, there will always be something new, so take the time to feel proud of what you have already achieved.

This is your entrepreneurial gap. You need to work to close it.

Be Passionate About Business, Not a Market

"A lot of entrepreneurs limit themselves to the markets they are passionate about. Personally, I'm passionate about business.

When we went into the survival and preparedness market, I wasn't that passionate about it. I don't even like camping, but I know that other people do.

I don't think you can remove passion from the process – someone will always be passionate. It just doesn't have to be you, so I see myself as a publisher, a producer, and owner."

– Ryan Deiss, founder and CEO of Digital Marketer

As Ryan says, he considers himself a producer and a business owner rather than the person who is passionate about a specific market. That kind of mindset shift will enable you to be passionate about business.

Producers do not have to learn to design and code – they need to take an idea and turn it into reality. Your job as a producer is to create something out of nothing.

A lot of entrepreneurs want to go into a market that they are passionate about, but either their passion doesn't align with a market that is hungry for a product, or it just limits them in some way. Ryan's passion is business, so he can enter any market and do really well... in business.

This is how I see it: if I can enter a market that is easy to make money in and build a good, solid business, I can use the money to buy time and freedom, and follow my passions.

Move from being a consumer to being a producer.

The Entrepreneurial Gap

The idea of the entrepreneurial gap has struck me so deeply that I have started to work this question into each of my interviews. Judging by the responses, the issue is definitely not mine alone.

Time is precious, and you are exactly where you need to be today. Everything you want will take time. No matter where you are six months or a year from now, know that you will still naturally project your success into the future.

This projection is inevitable and necessary to your growth, but it can also be devastating to constantly live in the gap between where you are and where you want to be.

This is as true for you, as it is for me.

Part III:

Ideas

Your Ideas Are Worthless, Until They Aren't.

Protected ideas are as good as dead, both yours and mine.

A lack of ideas has never been the reason we, as entrepreneurs, don't endlessly start new projects. Instead, it is due to a lack of resources, time, and energy within our personal lives and our organizations. Ideas breed more ideas, so even if right now you are struggling to come up with a great business idea, don't worry. We all need to come up with a long string of terrible ideas first.

Every business you see around you started from an idea that is either a slight variation of the founder's original idea, or a 180-degree pivot from the original idea. Ideas are the starting point, not the end goal: they get us thinking about products, services, markets, and prices, but the idea itself does not create a business.

Your ideas are worthless until you take action.

I do not need or want to steal your idea, and neither does anyone else that can help you. Trust me, your ideas just aren't that good, and neither are mine. At least not before we let them out into the world for others to bat around, tear apart, and possibly rebuild into solid business foundations.

Yes, it is terrifying to let your ideas out into the world. I get that. What if someone says it sucks? They will (I just did, and I don't even know what your idea is). No one ever said putting your ideas out into the world is easy – it's not. To this day, I cannot sleep for days before launching a new project.

Get used to it, or keep your day job.

There are people who have already made the mistakes you are about to make. Give them your ideas for feedback, discussion, and dissection. Maybe your idea is awesome, maybe it isn't – that's not the point. The point is, when you decide to give others the ability to destroy your ideas, then and only then will they achieve value.

It's cheaper, faster, and less frustrating to have them destroyed and rebuilt early on than to spend time, money, or effort on them first. Be open with ideas. When you begin to open up with your ideas, you will start talking to smart, interesting people that can help you.

If your ideas are as good as you think (and they will be if you come up with enough of them), others will notice and help you gain traction.

Now, let's jump into it.

Your Business Is Not about You

"The evolution of creatures depends on the ecosystem: animals adapt because that's what the ecosystem demands, not because they want to. The same thing applies to your ideas: it doesn't really matter what you want – it's about what the market wants. You have to listen to the ecosystem or you'll die.

Your business partially comes down to you and partially to the ability to destroy anything, no matter how good you feel about it.

You have a choice of whether something lives or dies, which is not based on how much you like it. It's based on how far it can jump, and how far it can jump is based on its ability to adapt.

The main point is to avoid emotional attachment and to be willing to destroy something at any time in order to rebuild it."

– Julien Smith, co-founder and CEO of Breather, and *The New York Times* bestselling author

Your business is not about you. Your business is about what the market and your customers want – and don't want. You need to remove yourself from this equation, so that the market can speak and you can listen with a clear, egoless mind.

Every idea that you have will not immediately be able to jump as far as it needs to. You will need to listen to the market and adapt to the feedback. The ability and willingness to destroy your ideas and rebuild them as necessary, is your ability to succeed as an entrepreneur.

Avoid the emotional attachment and don't take the feedback personally. Remember, it is not about you, but about your idea. Your job is to adapt your idea a thousand times until it can jump and scale itself through the marketplace.

Feedback is not failure. Adjustment is not defeat. It isn't you that failed, it's an idea – they are separate entities.

Your idea is not you.

Learn from Your Competition

"When you have a look at the best websites in your industry and compare them to yours, nine times out of ten you'll see straight away that your website is not as good as theirs.

You often don't have to ask people if they think something is a good idea, because you can just put a button and ask people to pay for it. If they do, you know it is a good idea."

– Dan Norris, co-founder of WP Curve and author of
The 7-Day Startup

Dan makes two awesome points here. First of all, stop worrying about your website, because you can simply learn from the best in your field. That's the advantage of working online: everything your competition does to be profitable is available to you.

Once you determine who the most successful companies are in your market, go to their sites, buy their products, and learn from their processes. Their pricing, product offerings, sales funnels, and opt-in offers are all available to you. Don't be shy. In order to win in your market, you need to understand your competition better than they understand themselves. Plus, you have the benefit of not having to reinvent the wheel – use the competition as a starting point and optimize from there.

Don't waste time asking people what plugin they prefer, because that is a stall tactic. It keeps you from doing what you're supposed to do and getting your product out there.

Dan started WPCurve on a $40 WordPress theme and a few years later had grown it to over $75k in monthly recurring revenue. He would never have done that without simply taking action. It is essential that you start moving on an idea as quickly as possible.

He compared himself to the best in his market. If you are going to emulate someone or get ideas from a site, don't go to the bottom of your market. Go to the top.

When I was creating HacktheEntrepreneur.com, I repeatedly went to *Smart Passive Income* by Pat Flynn. He is somebody I admire as a podcaster, blogger, and entrepreneur. He knows what he is doing and how to set things up. He has tested his ideas and processes with 100,000s of website visitors, and he's learned from his mistakes.

Secondly, allow people to pay you as a way of gaining information. I know people that came up with an idea over a weekend and literally put up a sales page with a buy button, to see if people would buy it, without the product or the service even existing yet.

The best thing is you can refund that person's money and tell them, "Glad you are so interested. What would you like from this product?" They can help you shape the product and will buy it again once you actually create it.

You can also do a pre-sale and tell them the product will be available in a month. There are no excuses, just start. As Dan said, you can easily get information without having to ask lots of people for their opinion.

Execute your ideas. Jump in.

Better to Try and Fail (Than Not Try at All)

"If I think something is interesting, I just do it, push it out there, and see what happens. Sometimes it works, sometimes it doesn't. If it doesn't work, at least I have tried it.

I don't want to end up at the age of sixty or seventy and see a pattern without acting on it. I tend to just go for it."

— David Meerman Scott, author of *The New Rules of Marketing and PR*

I am not worried about taking a shot and missing. I am not afraid of going after something that might not work out. I take shots in order to make my life better and do cool things every single day, rather than only trying something every now and then. Therefore, it doesn't matter if 80 or 90% of the shots don't work out, because I don't end up disappointed.

In order to have wins, you need to get through the failures. The problem with overthinking our ideas and waiting too long to take action is that the failures seem epic. If you plan to execute on one idea only, then the weight on that idea becomes too great.

Think about it this way: if you know that it will take you ten ideas before you find one that becomes profitable, yet you only execute one idea per month, how long will it take you to succeed? And even further, what are the chances that you would give up after eight months of defeat and never even get to the win?

Now, what if you took action on one idea per week or, if the ideas are small enough, one idea every day? Your time to success has shrunk to just days or weeks. The best part is, as soon as you hit that win, you will immediately forget about all the failures. Doesn't that sound better than giving up after month eight and never knowing what could've been?

I refuse to turn forty, fifty, sixty, seventy, or whatever, and look back to wonder what I could have done and achieved, what parts of the world I could have seen. I want to push everything in every way I can in order to do what I want. I refuse to care when I fail, and you can refuse as well.

There is nothing worse than regretting something you didn't try. You rarely regret doing something, but you do regret the things you didn't do. I refuse to not do something, because I want to know that at least I tried.

At least I tried.

Choose Themes, Not Goals

"We have no ability to predict our future, so it is important to have themes.

Jon's theme was to go to a mastermind in order to inspire and be inspired by smart people, which provided him with a variety of ways for self-improvement. That is a theme rather than a specific goal.

His theme led to him doing a podcast, which I'm sure he enjoys, or he wouldn't have done so many episodes."

— **James Altucher, who founded and co-founded over 20 companies, of which 17 have failed**

Themes rather than goals.

It's true we don't know where the future will lead us. I knew I wanted to create a new business, and my podcast ended up being that business.

James is right: I had no idea I was going to create it. I am quite sure that if I'd known what was coming, I would have become bored and lost my passion. As a result, I would have been unsuccessful. We can never know exactly where we are heading, but if we live and plan thematically, then we can at least start. Starting is the hardest part, and themes are the way to know in which direction to move – not exactly where you are going, but at least understanding the next step, for now.

I agree that we should be open, because we can't predict the future. However, having themes centered around what you want to do is a good thing. As James asks in his book, *Choose Yourself*, which I really recommend reading, do you want to choose yourself? Everything depends on what you choose to do. Themes are the best way to set yourself up for success as you see it.

Be Convinced You're Right (But Listen to Others)

"The other day, our head of communications, the CEO, and I were writing a blog piece. I was getting frustrated because I was convinced I was right – but they ended up improving my idea.

Afterwards, I told them, 'Please never let me end when I say I'm done. Carry on pushing me as hard as you can.'

If you feel you're the master of it all, you're not going to allow your team to push you. There are people in my office that are too smart for me not to listen to them. That way I won't win, and neither will the company."

– Benji Rogers, founder and President of PledgeMusic

Whether your ambitions are to build a massive company or a one-person business, it is crucial to surround yourself with smarter people who can help you and force you to grow. You have to be willing to listen to other people's ideas, while remaining stubborn enough to push ahead.

As Benji says, we have to be convinced we are right to a certain extent, in order to make things happen and create businesses. Coming up with an idea and creating something out of nothing takes a certain amount of "I'm right, goddammit." At the same time, however, we have to remain open to suggestions. Benji has advisors who can push him, but even solo entrepreneurs can surround themselves with people who will do just that.

This happened to me when I joined Rainmaker.FM. Until then I had been creating what I thought was a great show. People liked it, and it was doing well. At some point, it got the attention of Copyblogger and Rainmaker.FM, and I joined them. That transition really made me step up my game: I had to push the level of output up, which improved my show greatly, even without them saying that I had to. You have to push yourself to a certain level, and then find people to push you further.

If something doesn't make sense to you, ask the people around you, online or in your vicinity. Make sure to find people that will demand better of you, and will demand you to grow, learn, and push forward.

Find people that will push you as far as they can.

Pilot Your Idea

"A really important strategy I have used since the very beginning is piloting an idea. Try it on a small scale. See what works. See what doesn't work. Lower your risk. Experiment. Learn. Come back to the drawing table. Fix, adjust, and then decide whether or not to move forward."

– Kim Ades, founder of Frame of Mind Coaching

If I had had this conversation six months earlier, I would have skipped this part of the conversation, as it wouldn't have made much sense to me. However, after I started to work with Rainmaker.FM, which is part of Copyblogger Media, they asked me to create a podcasting course, for which they wanted a pilot version first.

I had never done a pilot version of anything before, but it made perfect sense: a bunch of people signed up, whose feedback allowed us to make the course exactly like they wanted, rather than us assuming what they wanted.

The idea of launching a pilot is to lower the risk and have the opportunity to fix, adjust, and move forward, or decide if it's even worth moving forward. That method can spiral into massive results.

When we created VelocityPage, we made a version 0.9. In terms of software, that is identical to a pilot, which I did not realize at the time. Normally, the first version is 1.0, but we didn't feel like we were ready for that. We didn't know how to proceed without letting the software out into the wild and getting feedback.

I wouldn't launch anything now without having a pilot first. It's a brilliant method that really lowers your risks and your barriers to getting started. Consider how you could execute a pilot launch for a select group of people.

Start small and start fast.

The Impact of an Idea Is in Its Implementation

> "In the startup world, people usually think ideas have a much higher value than they really do. The value of an idea is its impact once it is implemented."
>
> **– Eliot Peper, entrepreneur and author of Startup Fiction trilogy *The Uncommon Series***

We all have ideas that we consider million-dollar ideas, but they are useless until we do something with them. The value of an idea is only realized during its execution.

Whatever you do, don't covet your ideas. It bothers me when someone tells me, "I have a brilliant idea, but I can only tell you little bits of it." I'm not going to steal your idea. The reason I don't implement more ideas isn't due to a lack of ideas for businesses to start, but due to a lack of resources: I don't have enough time and people who can work with me. Even though the ideas are there, we can only do so much.

As James Altucher says, you should become an idea machine. Ideas are beautiful, but only once implemented. Your ability to come up with great ideas functions like a muscle – the more ideas you create, the easier it will be to create more.

You don't have to create a whole team around you – simply share your idea with someone else. They will run with it and create something cool, which will come back to you. Don't hold on to your ideas, but be someone who is known for coming up with great ideas and finding a way to implement them. After all, the value of ideas comes from their implementation, not their creation. Let's share our ideas with each other and create cool stuff with potential.

Ideas are not finite, so share them.

Don't Try to Be Something You're Not

"One of my friends told me that money is made by turning the wheel, not by reinventing the wheel. As I like reinventing the wheel, I'm constantly looking for people who are better wheel turners than me. If I create enough wheels and have enough wheel turners that are really excited about what we're doing, then that should be alright."

— Yanik Silver, founder of Maverick Business Adventure and Maverick 1000

People always try to come up with a grand million-dollar idea that is going to change a whole market. However, you don't have to reinvent the wheel. Implement something that works for another market in your own market, or find something that works in your market and adapt it to something unique. Put your perspective onto it. The idea of having to reinvent the wheel holds a lot of people back.

It's encouraging that Yanik disagrees with his friend's good advice: "That's great, but I *like* reinventing the wheel."

Yanik is smart and self-aware enough to know that he has to hire smart wheel turners, because he does agree that that is necessary for a successful business. He doesn't try to change himself or his strengths, because that is a futile endeavor. Work within your strengths and weaknesses, and put people into place around you to complement those traits.

Rather than struggling to become a wheel turner himself, he decided to continue doing what he is good at. Knowing full well that his role doesn't bring in all the money, he puts other people in place as wheel turners.

The money is made by turning the wheel.

Stop Living in the Dip

"A sure way to live in the dip for a long time is to half-ass your way through a project, doing it on the side.

If I want to try something, I want to get behind it properly and have the resources to do it well. That way, if it didn't work, I know that I gave it a good shot and I can decide what to do next.

People think the failure of a project is the worst thing, but it's not. The worst thing is being in no man's land, without knowing whether it was a failure or whether you did something wrong."

– Danny Iny, founder of Firepole Marketing and bestselling author

---

If you haven't read *The Dip* by Seth Godin, then please do. It's a short read about the struggle of pushing through. There's a sure way to live in the dip, which is the place you absolutely do not want to live in. Many of us do, however, because we don't want to put all of our time and effort into something. I don't know if it's because we're afraid of success or because we're afraid of failure, but we half-ass it.

Danny doesn't mean that you can't have a side project if you have a job. You can, but unfortunately you will have to work when you're not working your actual job or sleeping. There's eight hours between work and sleep in which we waste a lot of time. If we want something bad enough, we will focus and work those other eight hours until it succeeds.

The reason I build things out of nothing is that I don't want to be on my deathbed and wonder what I could have done. For example, I selfishly wanted to build *Hack the Entrepreneur* to talk to smart people and have cool conversations. When it started to draw an audience, I decided to push it as far as I could, because I wanted to see how far it could go. I didn't want to wonder three years later what could have happened if I had not half-assed it and gone for it flat out.

That is a decision you have to make at some point. The question is not whether you are making the wrong decision, but whether it turned out to be the right or wrong decision *after* you put in all the resources, time, and effort you could. If it doesn't work, it doesn't work, big deal. You know you pushed it as far as it could go. To me, that's a great place to be.

It's where you'll find happiness and success – however you want to define it for yourself. Make sure you're not continuously living in the dip because you're afraid to push it as far as possible.

Push hard and find what works.

Go Big

When you just get started, you will read a lot of crap online claiming that you should find yourself a niche. People will tell you to go super tiny, but I think the opposite is better. Go to a big market, like Neil says. If you joined the fitness market, for example, which is a multi-billion-dollar market, you could get only half a percent and still end up with a massive business.

However, if your niche was punk rock drummers that are digital entrepreneurs and run a podcast, it would be a badass book that I would read, but it is kind of ridiculous, because there are just not enough of us in the world to make it viable... at least not yet!

When I created *Hack the Entrepreneur*, I could have narrowed it down, but instead I went for entrepreneurship, because it allows a bigger audience. Yes, it's harder to get heard, to become known, and to create a business around. On the other hand, though, it's also easier in a lot of ways, because you're dealing with a lot more people and a larger scale of market.

When you are thinking about your business, listen to Neil. Go to the big markets and find a business within them. Don't go to a tiny market, because it's a lot easier to gain 0.5 percent of a market than it is to gain eighty percent of a market share in order to make a marketable business.

Go big.

Your Work Matters

Do you ever get the feeling that your ideas are not big or meaningful enough and what you are doing is not important?

You may feel like the websites you design or the headbands you make aren't changing people's lives, or further, aren't changing the world. In fact, your ideas and your work may feel so frivolous that you become ashamed and start to question why you do what you do.

When we think of work changing the world, we think of Steve Jobs. Mr. Jobs ran a company that sold a ton of products and changed how we consume music, and to some degree the web, but does that ultimately matter? One could argue that it's simply electronics cluttering up our lives and landfill sites. The world, although changed, would have been just fine without him. However, that in no way makes his work any less impactful, and the same goes for your work.

What you make in your business or your spare time, no matter how insignificant it may seem, has the ability to change someone's life. There is nothing more important. Changing someone's life usually starts in a small and insignificant way, with something as simple as making them smile – the significance comes after.

Let me explain. Since we are here right now, let's use this book as an example. Will writing these words directly change the world? Nope.

Does that mean I should stop writing? Nope.

There is a possibility that something you read in this book sparks an idea. You discuss that idea with a friend, and it evolves into something significant. Then, three (or more) steps away from these words, your friend does something with impact.

That is the goal. Always. Think three steps away from yourself.

It is not what you make, but how it makes someone else feel and think. Let's go back to the headband example. The goal of your headband is not simply to look nice; it goes much further than that, which is where your impact lies.

We do not buy nice clothes or accessories to protect us from the elements; we buy these items to look good. When we look good, we tend to feel better about ourselves and act more confidently. When we act confidently, we meet new friends that move our lives in new directions; we get new jobs and promotions at companies creating things with more levels of impact. Those new friends, jobs, and promotions are where your impact begins, not ends.

The end goal of your work should be to inspire a change in thoughts or feelings of your customer, audience, friends, and family. This rarely happens at the first step, but it does happen if we follow our work three steps away.

Your ideas and, therefore, your work matter to someone somewhere, and you have no idea what they may do with it.

Do what you do with the confidence of knowing it can and will change the world. The world may only be one person for one day, but is one person not worth it?

Please keep creating, building, crafting, writing, coding, drawing, knitting, and changing the world.

Part IV:

Being Wrong

Learning How to Be Wrong

As entrepreneurs, one of our greatest struggles is the fear of being wrong, making mistakes, and failing. If there was a way to attach an economic indicator to all the businesses and business ideas that do not exist due to fear, it would astound us.

This fear holds so much power because it is a self-fulfilling prophecy. New business ideas are left to die for fear of trying and failing, reducing the number of ideas that we ever put out into the world. We need to do the exact opposite in order to find success. More ideas, and more ideas that fail, will allow us to find the diamonds in the rough.

You cannot wait until that "million-dollar" (or is it billion-dollar now?) idea comes, and then act. Nevertheless, you need to act and implement your ideas constantly – that is where your greatest ideas lie.

It is hard to have your ideas destroyed. It's hard to not take personal offence at having your ideas torn apart, but you must – we all do.

This is not about whether or not you will succeed or fail. It is a fact that you will fail many more times than you will succeed – you must come to terms with that. I don't mean to destroy your ambition – quite the opposite in fact. This should empower you and reframe how you think about failure.

Failure is not the end of an idea or business venture, but the starting point of the next one.

Think about it this way: everything you have done (successes and failures) has led you to exactly where you are today. When you start a new idea and it fails, you can take a step back and learn from that failure. You now possess a new baseline for ideas and their implementation in the market, because you have learned what does not work.

Having an idea, implementing it, and letting the market tell you your idea was no good is not limited to those of us getting started in business. However, it is a mindset we need to adopt from the start of our entrepreneurial journeys if we are going to find and enjoy the successes we desire.

Think about Google for a moment, a massive company that has obviously had a lot of success. What about their failures? Google Reader, Google Glass, Google Notebook, Google Wave, and the soon-to-be Google Plus.

Are these product failures the sign of a business struggling to survive? No, the exact opposite, in fact. These are clear signs that Google is an impressive company. They understand very clearly that you have to continuously try new ideas, and let them be destroyed and counted as failures, in order to find the few ideas that will succeed. The same goes for each of us.

The way to deal with this constant state of failure and the brief glimpses of success is to nourish our abilities to deal with uncertainty in the outcomes of our ideas and businesses, in our markets and our customers' demands, and in our inevitable success or failure as entrepreneurs.

Uncertainty is the life-blood of an entrepreneur.

We can never imagine where our lives and businesses will lead us, and yes, that is a good thing. Everything in and around us and our businesses is constantly changing and evolving, which makes it impossible to predict the future.

What we can be certain of is that if we stick to wanting more out of life and knowing we have it within ourselves to do big things, then awesome things will unfold in front of us.

If it doesn't happen today, then keep working, stay focused, and you will see what tomorrow brings. Know that with uncertainty come unexpected promotions, partnerships, products, etc.

These things rarely come to those sitting around waiting for everything to be perfect and for all uncertainty to be removed from the equation. They only come to those of us who know for sure we need uncertainty.

The only way to fail as an entrepreneur is to quit before you've seen enough failures to find your success.

Now, let's jump into "Being Wrong" and how ten brilliant entrepreneurs deal with it.

The Best Way to Be Wrong

"I'm going to tell you the best way to be wrong.

When I have to close down a project I've been working on, I have to apologize to everyone that it didn't go the way I wanted it to go and feel bad about that. Afterwards, I can learn, which is the best way to be wrong.

What did I learn? What's good? What's bad? What can I really take from it?

The only way wrong ends up being bad is if you learn absolutely nothing. If you fail at something, remember you have to re-language failure to be an outcome you didn't expect."

– Chris Brogan, co-founder and CEO of Owner Media and *The New York Times* bestselling author of eight books

Not only are failure and being wrong inevitable in business and in life, but you should actively search for them and use them as a lesson. All forms of education have a cost tied to them – the cost of failure is time, resources, and humility. Yes, I agree: it's not always easy to make mistakes and fail, but it is absolutely essential.

When you make a mistake, it's not catastrophic. Keep moving, iterating, and using what you've learned to determine your next move.

Think about it this way: when you enter your bedroom in the dark, you reach for the light switch. If you miss, do you stop looking for it? Do you decide to wait for the sun to rise and provide you with light?

My guess is you would never think of doing that, because without even thinking, you take what you've learned (the light switch isn't where you just touched) and reach out to another spot on the wall. Again, if you miss a second and third time, you never think of living in the dark. You instantly reach out again: you don't get beaten by the defeat, and it never crosses your mind that you might not be cut out for living in a well-lit bedroom.

Think of your next business idea as a light switch.

Reinventing Business Education

"We grow up with the idea that failure is bad. If you get an F, you're not going to make it. Nothing can be further from the truth when it comes to entrepreneurship.

You *have* to fail.

I can teach you everything, but if you don't have your fair share of failures or at least a few cringeworthy experiences, you won't really grow."

– Omar Zenhom, co-founder of Business Republic and host of The $100 MBA

We are all aware that failure is essential to entrepreneurship, but we try to limit the damage.

I have generally been very lucky through hard work and determination, but the day before my interview with Omar I had the largest failure of my entrepreneurial career. I had been working on a seven-figure project, my biggest deal so far, for three months.

It was going to be great, but after two months of negotiation they walked away. I was devastated, but remembered what Chris Brogan had said about the need to internalize failures because they will be useful at some point.

You have to celebrate the wins and accept the losses. If this had happened to me a year earlier, I would have been depressed for a month, maybe longer. However, this time I just stopped working for the day and decided what to do. On the day of the interview, I woke up invigorated and ready to go.

You can celebrate your wins for a day, but not longer. In order to be really successful, you have to be able to work hard every single day, celebrating the wins and accepting the failures.

Let the big, powerful failures and losses hit you hard until the end of the day, and then learn from them. Part of being an entrepreneur is you can get punched by failure repeatedly, but you shouldn't give up.

The thought to go get a job never crosses my mind, because I know it's not in my DNA. I'm an entrepreneur.

Things suck sometimes, but that's part of the game – a game I love to play. Learn to love the game.

Own Your Mistakes

"If something hurts my income, I want it to be my fault. If my income goes up, I don't want it to be because I had to listen to someone else. I want to make my own mistakes and get there on my own.

You can't really succeed unless you make a lot of mistakes. In a job, you are punished for making mistakes. In your own business, you are actually rewarded, if you take the lessons to heart."

– Ben Settle, digital entrepreneur and email specialist

I love having the independence of being a digital entrepreneur, being responsible for myself, and taking ownership of my life. If I want to make more money, I can do that. If I don't make money, I only have myself to blame.

Complaining is not a strategy you can use to build a business. Own up to the fact that all of it, your wins and your losses, are the product of whether or not you worked hard enough on the right things.

Of course, you're still going to have non-stop failures, but taking ownership of them and moving forward quickly is the fastest and truest path towards success in business.

That doesn't just go for solo entrepreneurs – it is also one of the greatest traits of true leaders. A true leader knows and takes the blame for mistakes that happen within her team. She doesn't spend time or energy pointing fingers or placing blame on others – she steps up, takes fault, and finds a solution.

Own your mistakes.

Don't Struggle with Failure

"There is a difference between failure and your struggle with failure.

You do not have to struggle with failure. That is a choice on your part.

If you accept the fact that the person who fails the most wins, you can also accept that putting good effort into something that fails is a key part of your job."

– Seth Godin, digital entrepreneur and author of 18 bestselling books

Failure is something inevitable in business and in life, but somehow we seem better equipped to deal with it in day-to-day life. We start dealing with it when we learn how to walk, because falling is an essential part of the learning process. You have to fall again and again until you've learned how to walk. Giving up is not an option.

We should bear in mind that business works in the same way. Failing is part of the process of getting good at and mastering something. Making mistakes and dealing with your failures is part of your job as an entrepreneur.

Learning to fail and not allow it to sideswipe you is essential. Luckily, it is like a muscle in your body – the more you fail, the better you get. Failure is not catastrophic, it is simply a place to redirect and reiterate your project or ideas. We don't need to go back to where we started every time we bump into an obstacle, we only need to find a way around, over, or through the obstacle in our way.

Determine exactly what you want to accomplish and work back to where you are now. Once you have established the path to where you want to go, break it into as many smaller parts as possible. From there you can start working on the first step and continue until your path fails, then remap from where you are.

Be strong. Be wrong.

UGG Boots: An Incredible Vision

"You don't climb straight from nothing to something big. You hit an obstacle, climb over it, and reach the next level of the plateau. You cross the line again, cross another obstacle, and climb to the next level again.

The more you do that, the more you will look back and realize how far you've come. It is all about overcoming each obstacle as it hits and not giving up."

— Brian Smith, founder of UGG Boots

There is no such thing as smooth sailing. Nevertheless, when you fall while climbing an obstacle, you simply land back on the plateau you were just on. You don't have to start from scratch again.

When I was younger and read a lot of business books, I was fascinated by Donald Trump: he would build hotels and other buildings, go bankrupt, and then build the next "Taj Mahal", so to speak. How do you go from bankruptcy to that? It's simple: he fell back on the plateau he was just on and tried again. You don't have to start at the bottom once you've leveled up to the next plateau.

I have been playing the drums for about 20 years. If I go on a three-month trip, I don't play at all, but when I come back, I still know how to. I will probably be a bit rusty and some muscles won't work the way they are supposed to, but in a week or two everything will have come back.

That is a good way of looking at the obstacles you bump into: there is no issue with you, it is just how business works. By extension, it is how life works in general: everything seems to be going well until something sideswipes you.

The analogy of the plateaus is fitting, because you always just fall down to the previous plateau. The only struggle is getting onto the next one. Once you achieve that, you are safe there and only have to pound on the next obstacles. Brian knows this better than anyone, as he has had to deal with much crazier battles than most of us ever will. In spite of all the failures he experienced, he still came out creating a world-famous brand and business. That is work that matters.

Your failures are never catastrophic, so don't fear them.

Do Something Bold

"Failures in business are opportunities to be seized. If you don't fail at one point in your lifetime, you won't experience the ultimate feeling of success. True success comes from a ton of failures and learning from those.

As a result, you'll be able to make the right choices. I'm not a perfect person. I have made mistakes – as an entrepreneur, as a small business owner, as a human being – and will probably make a ton more. Learn from them and become even more successful."

– Nellie Akalp, co-founder of CorpNet

When something doesn't work, change it drastically to see what does work. The classic definition of insanity is doing the same thing over and over again expecting a different result. I see so many business owners who stick to a marketing or pricing plan because they have always done it that way and their business is doing okay. You need to test. Everything.

We live in a time in which we can build digital businesses that allow us scalability and freedom to work where and when we want. However, it is very important for our business's growth that we have the ability to test everything we do. Test every headline, price, guarantee, offer, etc.

As human beings and as business owners, we get stuck in our ruts. We do the same things over and over without thinking, until something happens. Nellie's business was about to fail, so she changed something and realized that 40% had just been added to her bottom line. It is necessary to do bold things as a rule, not just when you are going out of business. Test everything and contemplate what your business could be.

Even if your business is doing okay, you could do something bold. The worst-case scenario is that you go back to doing exactly what you were doing before, so it is always worth a shot. The upside is that you never know until you test.

Test and change. Scale and grow.

Investing in Projects to Relieve the Itch

"People make money to buy expensive cars, big houses, etc., but I don't have a lot of those vices.

I prefer to spend my money on new projects and businesses. At the end of the day, even if a business fails – and God, I've had a lot of failures – it has satisfied my itch and I felt good doing it. If it doesn't work out, that's cool.

You can't be great at everything – on to the next!"

– Sol Orwell, co-founder of Examine.com

Sol touches on two major topics in this hack.

First of all, the idea is not to splurge on fancy things – at least not yet. A lot of people want to leave their comfortable job, but have too many expenses to take the leap into entrepreneurship. At some point, you will have to cut back on expenses in order to make a business scale up, above anything you've ever made before.

To be clear, I am in no way telling you to cut back on business expenses or not allow yourself to buy a latte while you work at the coffee shop. You are now in business, so it is always smarter to determine your expenses and then find new customers to pay you, so you can cover those expenses.

It kills me when I see someone with a software business researching the best deal on a new laptop for hours or days. Buy the best one, write off the cost against your business, and spend that time selling software to pay for the laptop and more.

Rather than indulging himself with fancy, shiny things, Sol invests his money in new projects.

That is exactly how I function: I enjoy putting my money into new projects and new experiences, like traveling. I travel lots with my family and for business, because that is why I have a business. Those things really allow me to find happiness.

The second point is that Sol embarks on new projects to scratch his own itch. It is something he really wants to do, so he doesn't get bothered if a project doesn't take off. It doesn't matter, because at least he gave it a try.

Always be proud of creating something out of nothing.

To me, that is a huge success. Even if you don't make a bunch of money out of it, you have done something most people in the world will never do and you deserve a pat on the back. You have executed your ideas, which gives them value.

Money is a renewable resource, time is not.

You Don't Need Permission to Be an Entrepreneur

"When a baby is learning to walk, they constantly fall over, but that doesn't make them want to stop trying. They don't think, 'That's it, I'm done with walking. I look stupid, everybody is laughing at me. I will just crawl from now on.'

As human beings, we are not naturally afraid of looking stupid or failing. We get educated into it."

– Steli Efti, founder of Close.io and Elastic Sales

This is by far the best analogy I have heard about how to be comfortable being wrong. When a baby does not yet know how to walk, they won't stop trying after falling down a few times.

We are not born afraid of failure, but we are taught to be embarrassed by it. We could point fingers and blame others for instilling this fear within us, but where would that get us? Step up to the plate and know you are not alone – we have all had the fear of the unknown and failure instilled in us from an early age. The good news is, we can and must overcome these fears.

If I had given up on business when my first three businesses failed, I wouldn't have been writing this for you. If I had not pushed through the first podcast I started and nobody listened to, then I wouldn't have started *Hack the Entrepreneur* and built it into the platform it is today.

Looking back, the failures seem insignificant and trivial, but at the time a few of them seemed devastating. I am not going to tell you they won't feel that way for you too, but trust me when I say that on the other side of those failures is a great place to live, work, and play.

We are all in this together and we all have the same fears to overcome. They still get me daily, but I know I have to push through them. You need to adopt this attitude. Do not waste even a minute complaining or passing blame to where these fears came from. Focus on working through them.

Complaining is not a strategy.

Grow by Working Through the Dips

"You don't often see progress in a straight line. It's not like a hockey stick, where everything starts down here and just zooms up to the top.

You tend to see some progress from last month to this month, and then maybe to next month, after which maybe things will tail off a while. You might even drop down a little bit in the following month.

If you keep measuring over time, however, you'll notice it actually is an upward trend. Don't get discouraged just because things don't do as well one month."

– Anita Campbell, founder and CEO of Small Business Trends

Anita's point truly hits home. I hope I have never misled you into thinking my guests and myself have followed a hockey stick growth in our businesses, because that is not how it works. Quite the opposite, in fact.

I have repeatedly discussed the concept of the "dip", coined by Seth Godin. The concept refers to the fact that everything in life or in business that's worth doing will start going up, make it seem like the sky is the limit, and then drop off into the dip. The harder that dip is and the longer it takes to get through, the bigger the rewards are on the other side. This is due to the fact that most people give up just before completing the dip.

As Anita says, you have to bear in mind the vision of working on projects in months and thinking longer term. You cannot start something today and expect it to simply take off, but you have to work through the dips.

As trends sometimes fall month to month, you have to take a step back and look at the bigger picture, which will show you an upward trend. The same thing happened with *Hack the Entrepreneur*. If I hadn't taken Seth's advice and looked at the long-term trend line, I would have quit around episode

50, because for months it seemed like nobody was listening.

At the beginning of the show, there were a lot of listeners. Then it fell off, and I pushed through. That stadium took about three months, and then it really started to skyrocket again. Most people would have quit at that point. The show has now grown to the point where more people listen to my show daily than the amount that used to listen in a month. That's the benefit of pushing through the dip.

We all go through the dip, not just you. Every single one of the more than 200 entrepreneurs that have been on my show has been through it and will go through it again, repeatedly.

When you find yourself in the dip, put your head down, keep working, and don't look up until it's clear you've made it through.

If My Business Fails, It's Because I Suck

"There's no middle ground. Something either worked because it worked out, or it failed because I wasn't good enough. That's okay.

I have to be okay with the possibility that everything could fall apart, even if I do everything I can to make this company happen.

If it fails, it's probably because I suck."

– Austen Allred, founder of Grasswire

Saying something failed because we suck sounds really harsh, but it is absolute ownership.

It is important that we take ownership of everything that happens to us – not just in the companies we build, but in our entire lives.

Even though many situations are out of our control, we can't just sit there worrying about what could go wrong.

Moreover, we can't blame others when something happens to us. We are responsible – solely.

When we decide to put ourselves out there by creating a product, service, or startup, we have to be aware that everything comes down to us. We are putting ourselves on the line. By doing that, we allow ourselves to succeed while owning the responsibility, just like Austen did.

You got this. If you don't, own it.

The 24-Hour Reset

We know that in order to be successful, we must not let failure hold us back. It's all part of the process. We've heard it. We know. We know. WE KNOW.

When we stumble, we know we need to get back up and try again. No one is born knowing how to walk, yet we learn eventually, by not quitting. But what happens when we win a huge client or launch a new product? We may go out for a celebratory beer. There is nothing wrong with that, except when it becomes an excuse.

When we are still basking in the glory of a win five days later, that in turn ends up being as hard on our businesses as if we had failed.

Let's try something I call the 24-hour reset.

Every win. Every loss. Every positive. Every negative. All of it gets discarded every 24 hours.

You launched your new product today. Congratulations! Today, you can pat yourself on the back and congratulate yourself on a job well done. But today only. Tomorrow you are starting afresh and need to create a new win.

From now on every day, whether it was awesome or awful, is celebrated or learned from – then reset.

Your mistakes and failures only count long enough for you to learn from them (and hopefully not make them again). Your successes are celebrated (of course) but never allowed to diminish tomorrow's hustle. You need that hustle to create more wins.

This is a simple (though not easy) mindset shift that will allow you to start seeing the effects of compound growth through repeated wins and diminished losses.

Celebrate today, if it's worth celebrating. You deserve it.

If it's been one of those days where nothing seems to be going right, don't worry, because tomorrow you hit reset.

Go forth and reset.

Part V:

Growth

Your Growth Will Come From Within

In order to grow your business, you must first grow as an entrepreneur and as a person. The ability to scale your ideas and efforts takes leverage, which can only be gained through self-awareness and getting out of your own way. This is where most entrepreneurs fail.

Nourishing self-awareness will enable you to discover your strengths, but – more importantly – also your weaknesses.

Entrepreneur after entrepreneur that I have spoken to can look back on a defining moment in their business – a time when they realized true growth. That time is pinpointed to when they learned how to take a step back from their own thoughts and actions, in order to determine exactly what they are not good at in their business. Those weaknesses need to be delegated to people whose strengths are your weaknesses. That is where you will find growth.

Like so many other parts of your business, growth comes as much from your mindset as it does from your actions. Action is essential and will get you quite far, but not to the point of finding true scale in your business. True scale is when you begin to build something far bigger than yourself.

Now, let's jump in and find some growth for you and your business.

Find Your Multiplier Effect

"If you want unlimited income, you're going to have to piggyback and find a multiplying effect.

I was fascinated by the question, 'How can I find this multiplying effect that doesn't require my presence?' My journey has been to find a way to piggyback on other opportunities, so I can keep my freedom to do what I want. Working for somebody else was never going to work for me, ever."

– Stephen Key, entrepreneur, inventor, and bestselling author of *One Simple Idea*

I never actually thought of it in this way before, but Stephen is absolutely right. Passive income refers to scalability, not to sleeping all day. Scalability to me is absolutely essential in building a business, because it goes hand in hand with the multiplier effect. Personally, I do this in two ways: through my podcast and my software products.

I can create something like my podcast once and put it out there, after which it can multiply and literally get listened to by tens of thousands of people around the world. That's amazing! Instead of me going and knocking on a door, shaking hands with somebody and meeting them, I create a multiplier effect, which is absolutely essential. That is how you should see passive income and the way it's created. Do things that can scale and become bigger than you could ever make them.

I achieve the same effect when creating software products, like VelocityPage. Even though I have to do ongoing development and maintenance, I basically build the product and that's that. Whether I sell one or a hundred software licenses a day does not influence my workload. That is absolute scalability.

I fully agree with Stephen: if you want unlimited wealth and the potential of being able to take yourself out of the equation at some point, you need to find that effect. It is impossible to achieve it when you work for somebody else. That other person, the owner of the company, will be the one who gets the multiplier effect.

Understanding the Math of Success

"If you believe somehow you're set to a certain capability and level of accomplishment, then you'll never achieve anything more. However, if you believe you can get better and do other things, that growth mindset will enable you to accomplish more."

– Guy Kawasaki, entrepreneur and *The New York Times* bestselling author of thirteen books

The growth mindset really needs to be clarified, as it is essential to you becoming the successful entrepreneur you want to be and doing the things you want to do. If you believe you are somehow limited to a certain capability or level of accomplishment, then you definitely will be.

You need to have what Guy calls "the growth mindset", which is the mentality that you can teach yourself to do anything if you push yourself hard enough and try enough things.

This idea has been further explored and validated by Carol Dweck in her classic book *Mindset*.

What's the best way to create a successful business? Go out and start ten in a row. One of them will succeed, or you've at least put the odds in your favour. It's very rare that the first song a musician writes becomes a hit, so don't think the first business you start needs to be a success. Have the mentality that out of the ten you started, only the tenth one will be successful.

Don't start a business, put everything into it, fail, and then think you're not an entrepreneur. You are. You simply need to have the growth mindset and bear in mind that, if you put in the effort, you will become an entrepreneur.

Entrepreneurs are not born – they are created through mindset, determination, and a willingness to work hard.

Guy has proven that time and time again. I'm so glad that he brought this up and took us back to the very beginning, because it's really essential. Have a growth mindset. Know that you can teach yourself and learn. Your capabilities are only limited by your willingness to work hard at them.

Hard work + willingness to fail = success.

Be Proud, Yet Unimpressed

"Part of being an entrepreneur is being able to hold multiple scenarios in your head simultaneously.

For one, I'm very proud of what I've done, but simultaneously I am very unimpressed by it. Because that's what being an entrepreneur is all about. It's moving forward, and I'm very grateful for all the people I've worked with. They've really changed my life, and I've done my best to help improve theirs.

By the time one of your dreams finally happens, it's so over, it's so old. Like, a new thing is the next three-year thing.'"

– Paul Anthony Troiano, founder and CEO of Rumblefish

Paul makes a brilliant point about "the entrepreneurial gap", which I would like to dive into a bit more.

We are always forward-thinking and forward-looking, which is not necessarily a problem. The problem is we don't stop to look behind us, so as to congratulate ourselves or be humbled by what we have accomplished.

Paul's idea of entrepreneurship is "holding multiple scenarios in your head simultaneously": he's both humbled and unimpressed by what he has accomplished. That's perfect, since it means he understands the gap.

You have to appreciate what you've accomplished, no matter how small it might seem, while remaining unimpressed, because that will drive you forward.

As entrepreneurs we have a tendency to set a goal, accomplish it, and immediately replace it with five more ambitious ones.

I am not saying we, as entrepreneurs, shouldn't dream, push ahead, and throw our goals into the future – it's absolutely necessary for us to do that. Nevertheless, we also need to be aware of the gap between pride and being unimpressed by what we have accomplished.

The Extraordinary Value of Sharing and Being a Connector

"I have tips and resources that I want to share, and I don't want to wait for a publishing platform to give me permission. Nobody told us we had to wait to do anything – we could just put our ideas out there, which was really a huge game changer.

My husband didn't think anyone would care about all the resources I was throwing online, but they did. Our readers have been incredibly faithful to us over the years.

I have always found that oversharing pays off in readership. Hence, I don't save my best tips for myself, but I share them on all our social media platforms."

– Nicole Feliciano, founder and CEO of MomTrends

There is no such thing as oversharing: Nicole has built her complete business on sharing.

A crucial part of blogging and building any business online is not waiting for permission to share our best stuff. We have to share everything we know, without keeping the best things to ourselves.

James Altucher made a similar point: we should become idea machines and share our ideas with others. If we can't do anything with a certain idea, we can give it to somebody else. By letting our ideas go, we allow more to come back to us.

Everyone has something they know better than most people. That might be hard to believe about yourself, but there is something. For me personally, it could be playing drums in a rock band. There are tons of other drummers who may know more than me, but I have my own unique take, and so do you. That is your uniqueness. Don't hide or suppress it – nourish it and let the true you come through in everything you do.

Nicole mentions her husband didn't think anyone would care. Instead of listening to him, she decided to build the Momtrends media empire and share her tips in order to help people.

Helping and sharing is content marketing, which is how you build a business nowadays. Build an audience, then determine what they need from you. Create content, find your audience, build your business. Please do not fall into the trap of building a product or service, and then trying to find customers – that is a recipe for disaster.

Her very best tips are shared by a whole team that promotes them as heavily as possible. The reasoning is that if you keep giving, you will get back at some point. It might take a while, like it did for Nicole, but once it comes, it will do so in an impressive way.

Give everything you can give. Don't hold anything back.

Be the CEO of Your Show

"You have to give yourself the time to be CEO, even when running a one-man show. If you don't, you won't grow."

– Brian Clark, co-founder and CEO of Rainmaker Digital

This touches upon a recurring problem entrepreneurs, both new and seasoned, experience.

When you're running a one-man show, it can be very difficult to position and visualize yourself as the CEO. It can feel rather silly: "CEO of what? Myself?"

Yes, it is necessary to take the time to create the content that will build your business. Nevertheless, you will not see massive growth without becoming the CEO and thinking about the big picture, so you can figure out what you have to do next for your business to grow.

It happens so often, offline and online, that people get stuck in their business and don't grow for years, because they are busy doing other things. I have been guilty of it myself, and I still struggle with focusing on delegation and embracing a forward-thinking vision.

Being busy is not good if you are not working on the right problems. This requires stepping back, thinking like a CEO, and being strategic with your limited time and resources. That is where growth will come from within your business. There really is no other way to scale.

Brian has obviously managed scalability, as he turned a one-man blog into an eight-figure business with a team of 50+ people spanning the globe. He is someone I have personally learned a lot from, and you should too.

Be the CEO of your show.

Learn to Think Big

"You have to learn to think big and small. You have to go in the same direction with small day-to-day decisions, as well as big actions.

Once you are on your way, you will mostly have to occupy yourself with little things, which can be tedious. Nevertheless, you are the one who has to do them right."

– Gabriel Weinberg, founder and CEO of DuckDuckGo

Gabriel's observation brings clarification to something I talk about regularly. As founders and entrepreneurs, we have to find the one or two things we are really good at, so we can accentuate them and make them into what we are about. We can get other stuff off our plates by delegating and hiring people.

However, at the same time it is necessary for us to be able to do everything ourselves, especially at the beginning. When I started my podcast, I did every single thing myself: editing, promotion, copywriting, website maintenance, finding and booking guests, etc. Then, I came to the point where I had enough money coming in to hire an editor, a graphic designer, a web developer, and an assistant.

It is great to be able to outsource certain aspects, but a business doesn't start out that way. You can't run a business in deficit, spending money that doesn't have any revenue.

For three months I had to work really hard to achieve the podcast and do things that are not my forte. Many entrepreneurs prefer focusing on the big picture and are not very good at the nitty gritty aspects or the fine details.

However, that is what makes us entrepreneurs: at times, we have to do the work that has to be done, even if we're not great at it and don't like doing it. It is the nature of running a business.

Think big and work small.

Define Your Perfect Day

"How do you know if you need money? The answer is simple. When you believe you can potentially scale a business or problem in a seven-year period to 100 million in revenue, then you may be in a good spot to raise venture capital.

The other thing is there's a high probability that if your business is successful, you will own a very small percentage of the company. The Mark Zuckerbergs of the world are very rare. More likely, you will never be financially rewarded from your startup.

I feel that people overvalue raising capital, with regards to living the ideal day. People say they want to be rich, but they don't. What they want is the ideal day, and that's where you should start with regards to why you are doing what you are doing."

– Dan Martell, founder of Clarity.FM

This is the simplest and most clearly defined answer to the question of funding I have ever heard. You no longer need to waste any time, thought, or energy wondering if your business (or business idea) needs funding to succeed.

Get started, determine your unit economics, and project your scalability over the next seven years. Be honest with yourself, if this is the game you want to play. Starting and running a venture-backed company is not for everyone. It's not even for most people – yet I know it has crossed the mind of every entrepreneur out there, at one point or another.

Dan goes on to mention the perfect day as you envision it, and the importance of knowing what you want out of your business and, ultimately, your life.

Wherever and however you decide to grow and scale your business, do it with an end goal in mind of the perfect day. How does it look? What and who is involved in making it perfect?

Your business can and should become anything you imagine it to be. Clearly define what you want out of your business, and then go create the business that enables you to live that life. As spiritual entrepreneur, philanthropist, and teacher John Assaraf states, "Ask not if you are worthy of your goals, ask instead, is your goal worthy of your life."

Define your perfect day.

Projecting the Introspective Mindset

"When you lead a team and create something out of nothing, which is what entrepreneurs do and thrive upon, you should do it in the most effective and efficient manner possible. A lot of the time that means being introspective of your strengths and constantly hacking to get better at what you do."

– Chris Myers, co-founder and CEO of BodeTree

As human beings and entrepreneurs, it is essential that we practice introspection to understand our strengths and weaknesses. This introspective thought creates self-awareness, which is necessary to our growth and success as entrepreneurs. We need to have the ability to not only know our strengths, but to also hold a firm grasp on our weaknesses.

Understanding our weaknesses is a way for us to better grow ourselves and our businesses. Any entrepreneur that feels they are good at everything, is deceiving themselves, as well as getting in the way of their business's growth.

This self-awareness also enables us to act more confidently. Deep down we all know we cannot and do not have to be good at everything – in fact, just having one or two key strengths is more than enough. Looking inward at our weaknesses not only allows us to admit them, but also to nourish them and realize we need to replace ourselves in those areas.

Our businesses do not need us to be good at everything, but they do require us to acknowledge our shortcomings with courage and humility.

It is your weaknesses (as much as your strengths) that define you.

From Good to Bored to Great

"A lot of people quit when they're tired. An entrepreneur should only quit when they're done."

– Oren Klaff, founder of Intersection Capital and author of *Pitch Anything*

The ability to not quit when you are tired, bored, upset, defeated, broke, stumped, or exhausted to the point of not being able to get out of bed will be the defining characteristic for whether or not you build a business that changes your life and the lives of others. Only quit when you are done.

Having six-figure product launches, making money while we sleep, and flying to conferences to network with smart, successful people – that's what we think of when we think of business. What about testing, hiring (and firing), endless meetings, spreadsheets, copywriting, writing content for the blog, contracts, lawyers, accountants, and more content creation?

Is there anything less exciting than lawyers and accountants?! Nope, there isn't. This is where we get bored. These are the parts of running a business that cause us to lose interest and fail, even though they are some of the most important aspects of a successful business.

It has been stated that the difference between the best athletes in the world and everyone else is the former's ability to deal with boredom.

When everyone else gets bored of doing the same exercises and drills, the ones who persevere become the experts in their fields. Your biggest hurdle to doing what you love full-time is your ability to keep your ass in your chair when it feels like work.

Your ability to deal with boredom is directly related to your ability to succeed.

Running your business is the same: the people who can work through their boredom and get the things done that need to be done, are the ones who succeed.

We are rarely born great. We need to show up day in and day out, work through the boredom, and be ready for greatness on the other side. Going from good to bored to giving up is easy. We know this, because we have all done it at one point or another.

This book itself has sprung from me interviewing 200 entrepreneurs. I'm a drummer. Drummers don't talk into microphones. I have always hated the sound of my voice when recorded. When I interviewed Chris Brogan for the first episode of *Hack the Entrepreneur*, I had never interviewed anyone before.

When you add hating the sound of one's voice to zero interviewing experience, would you think I would succeed as a podcaster? I refused to not know how to interview, because I knew I needed to talk to these brilliant entrepreneurs if I was going to fulfill my own dreams. I pushed myself and worked my ass off until I went from bad to good, good to bored, bored to great.

People like Oren will only be interested in investing in you if they know you won't stop when you're tired or knocked down one too many times. Investors know a business will only succeed if its owner has the right mentality – the business idea matters, but the success of the business comes down to the owner's ability to not quit until their jobs are done.

Go from good to bored to great.

Work Your Ass Off

"I want to make clear that all my success has come out of hard work. Hustling is nothing new. It's been around for decades, and we should just call it 'working our asses off'. That's what you need to do if you want to be a successful entrepreneur."

— Chris Ducker, founder of Virtual Staff Finder and Live2Sell. He is also the bestselling author of *Virtual Freedom*

If you outwork other people, you will succeed.

Before starting with *Hack the Entrepreneur*, I didn't know how to run a podcast and had never interviewed anyone in my life.

Nevertheless, most other people with a podcast quit before me or never started in the first place, because they had no experience either. Others decided to publish one episode per week, because doing three (like me) was too much work.

The reason why I got this far and you are now reading this book, is that I outwork most people. That's how simple it is.

I am not better, but I am getting better, because I do more than others. I used to be afraid of talking into a microphone, but now it's what I do most of the day. I used to not be able to sleep for days before launching a new product – what if it sucked and nobody cared? Okay, to be fair, I still freak out a little before launching something new, but that's part of the fun.

I have no delusions of super powers or holding any special abilities. Simply stated, I outwork most people, and that's exactly what you have to do too.

You don't have to outsmart your competition or have more resources, you just have to outwork them. It all depends on how badly you want something compared to the next person. You can't achieve your goal without wanting it and working harder for it than the person next to you.

So please, determine what you want and where you want to be a year from now. Work back the steps that need to be done, and then outwork the next person. Talk to me in a year from now and if you wish, you can thank me for giving you the necessary kick in the ass.

It's not easy – there's no magic pill, sorry. You have to outwork the next person. This isn't some new thing that was invented with the term "hustle". It is an essential step in your growth as an entrepreneur. Work your ass off.

When you do, it will be awesome and inspiring to watch.

There Is No Secret

We see the sudden success of others, and think we must be doing something wrong or are undeserving of that level of success.

What we don't see is the four, five, or ten years of hard work that took place before the overnight success. We don't see it, because it isn't glamorous or sexy. Most importantly, we don't see it because it removes instant gratification.

We want to believe the entrepreneurial lottery exists and we may get lucky one day when our number comes up. That is not how it works.

Nothing beats ass-in-chair working, or going out banging on doors and drumming up business. It's the hard workers that prevail. Always.

I am reminded of a quote from a brilliant writer that suddenly passed away recently, David Carr. David was often asked what his secret was to becoming a great writer. His answer was always the same: "Keep typing until it turns into writing."

Inspiration comes when you do the work, and success comes after years of making mistakes, failing, and not giving up. Keep writing until you get good. Keep building businesses until one of them works.

It only takes one real success to truly change your life. What you are working on right now or thinking of starting, could be that success. So get to it.

Conclusion

(and Guarantee)

What to Do Next

There are two things I would love for you to remember after reading this book.

First of all, live in days. Work in months.

You want to build something big that has the potential to change the life you live, yet you jump around from one idea to the next, without getting any closer to your goals. Whenever you come up with a great idea for a new business, excitement and emotion take over. You jump headfirst into your new project, only to lose momentum after a few days.

Remove emotion from the equation.

Anything life-changing and worth your time will take you months to accomplish, whether you think so or not. Building a business is not a lottery – you can't buy a ticket and suddenly be successful.

That is why thousands of people every day launch podcasts, blogs, and new products, without ever achieving any real success. They hope the launch will be their lottery ticket, and when it isn't – which it never is – they give up on their idea.

When you plan in advance to work in months, you remove your own expectation of instant gratification. At the same time, you prepare yourself to settle in and get to work for the next few months.

Every project will have a different length of time to completion, but that's not the point. Nothing worth doing will take you less than months of work to see real results, whether you are starting a podcast, building a blog, or developing software. You will be working in months, not just until you launch, but also while building a meaningful audience and business.

Planning to work in months will set you on a path to not only working in months, but also to vacationing and traveling in months. That is the beautiful byproduct of a project-based business and lifestyle.

The second point I would like you to take from this book is to go ahead and try.

Remember there are no guarantees.

"On the day I die, I'll say at least I fucking tried. That's the only eulogy I need." – Frank Turner, *Eulogy*.

My life is dictated by this sentiment, and I hope that yours will be too. Constantly take action on ideas, passions, and things you want to accomplish. Build things that matter. Use your momentum to encourage great things out of life.

I want to create products that make people's lives better, podcasts that encourage others to start businesses and live life on their terms, and write books that cause a ripple effect among brilliant entrepreneurs like yourself.

Do I succeed 100% of time? Nope, not even close.

In fact, doing some quick math and switching to a basketball analogy (for no apparent reason), I realize I hit about two out of every ten shots I take.

But you know what?

I take shots every day.

Every. Day.

Can I guarantee you will succeed? Nope, and even if I could, what would be the fun in that?

I refuse to not try. I refuse to not fail. I refuse to sit on the side lines.

This is who I have become. This is how I play the game. Life is short; you might as well play as hard as you can.

It can look easy from the outside, but I haven't always been like this.

I spent years spinning my wheels, getting no traction, and failing to make the changes that would allow me and my family to live a better life.

But no more.

Perhaps it's age, or perhaps I've learned to stop caring about whether something will work or not.

You know what absolutely will not work?

Not trying something because you are too scared. Guaranteed.

About the Author

I'm Jonny Nastor. I am digital entrepreneur, podcaster, writer, and punk rock drummer. I like my businesses like I like my music: loud and independent.

I make my home online at HacktheEntrepreneur.com and I write a new hack each week for my newsletter. You can (and should) join it on my website.

You can connect with me on Twitter at @JonNastor, and you can email me at jon@hacktheentrepreneur.com if you feel so inclined.

Acknowledgments

To Mom: Thank you for your unwavering support through everything I've ever attempted to do. I hope this book makes it easier to explain to your friends how I make my living.

To Dad: Thank you for teaching me that there are ways to make a living outside of the traditional (and boring) path.

To Andres and Nathan: Our conversations not only keep me sane, they also push me to new heights. For this, I thank you.

To Nick Davis: Thank you for all early morning conversations and late night website emergencies. You are a true friend and one day soon we will meet in person.

To Jennifer Schoen: Thank you for stopping me when I wanted to scrap this whole book idea. You've made this book better than I could have and I am happy to call you a friend.

To Jerod Morris: Thank you for teaching me the importance of becoming a Showrunner and encouraging me to write this.

To the Rainmaker.FM family: Thank you for taking me under your wings, pushing me to do good work, and putting up with me. You rule.

Made in the USA
San Bernardino, CA
11 April 2016